Wounded, Widowed & Winning

Turning your Trauma into Triumph

By Vioree Brandon-Nettlesford

Unless otherwise indicated, Bible quotations are taken from New King James Bible (NKJV). Copyright © 1982 by Thomas Nelson, Inc.

ISBN 9 78-0-578-885212-4

Dedication

This book is dedicated to all wounded widows and widowers who've chosen to take this journey with me. This is a plight that no one desires or asks for. It is one that is thrust upon you unwillingly. For many of us, one of the hardest things to do is exposing our wounds by way of revealing our scars and the shattered pieces of our lives for the pursuit of purpose. Always remember, your story has been assigned to your purpose, which has been designed to produce healing for those you will come into contact with. Nothing is by accident. You may not understand all that has happened until this very moment but keep living! Allow God to continue to process you. I guarantee you; your pain turns into POWER when you plug into the source of your Purpose! It will all make sense.

"When you find the courage to tell your story, make sure you tell it with the conviction that you only survived because of God's grace which allowed you to be called an overcomer."

-Vioree Brandon-Nettlesford

Preface

Writing "Wounded, Widowed, and Winning" was absolutely necessary for me as I embarked on my healing journey to release the pain of lifelong complex traumas. As I scribed the pages, this literary work became much more than a therapeutic release; it helped me to identify triggers and fostered my continued healing so that I could become the winner that stands before you today. I walked a road of trials in order to share my triumphant testimony. Reliving the memories disclosed in each chapter pained me like the birth of a natural baby without an epidural. I felt every emotion and endured pains in my stomach reliving the dread of that life-changing day... going home to tell my children their dad was never coming back. I had to face the looming unfulfillment of trying to move on with my life and not being satisfied because he was no longer there to touch me or hold me. I felt the absence of hearing his voice and was reminded of the loss of being overjoyed by his laughter. The pain in these pages is very real, very tangible.

This is my written testimony of how we, widows, triumph against all odds. There were many days throughout my writing process where the tears fell uncontrollably, but I knew that I had to birth everything that God had put in me to help others overcome the trauma of widowhood. However, my story began long before widowhood. Even as a young girl, I felt like I was doomed to fail. For many years through adolescence and into young adulthood, I was in a perpetual state of depression and did not know how to get out of that cycle. That cycle was broken the day I made a decision to live. Not for my children, or those that were looking up to me, but I made the decision for me. Despite the many layers of grief and longing, I was determined to live. I needed to (and desperately wanted to) learn to love me. I also desired the love and touch of my deceased husband. But more than that I wanted the touch of the Father to totally heal me. I needed healing from the memory of the traumas of my childhood, adolescence and now as an adult.

It was not easy to reveal the wounds within exposing my struggles and the vulnerable matters of my heart. I was challenged by this call and wanted to give up many times. The questions that sparked a fire in me to keep writing despite my tears and which encouraged me to push to complete this project were:

"Who am I supposed to reach by my experiences?"

"Who are the women that are assigned to me by God?" These questions fueled that fire to define the many facets of who I thought I was before my trauma, who I was after, and who I wanted to become.

My purpose is to sow seeds of hope, restore joy, and be a living reminder that all isn't lost. While empowering women to know healing is available once they have found your voice. I found my voice the moment I took the limits off of my story which was the turning point that helped me find my voice. Finding who I was and what I was created to do has been the catalyst to the discovery of my purpose. I've learned that your voice is the portal to finding your purpose. Once I discovered purpose, I knew the power that was attached to every word I spoke.

Now, let's ask ourselves, what does finding your voice look like? Sound like? What are the attributes of this woman who has found her voice? I do believe everyone's process of finding their voice varies. I am what some would call a "tough cookie to crack". In my process, I realized that I was very stubborn. I did what I wanted to do, how I wanted to do it, and in the time frame in which I believe it should be done. I gave no room for growth or change. I've learned the hard way that my stubbornness was my greatest hindrance to essential change. Change is necessary and ultimately, it is inevitable. Where there is no change, there is no growth. Where there's no growth, it becomes a dead end and people don't want to hang around dead places or things. For that reason, my process was lonely and extremely depressing. In hindsight I see my stubbornness was the cause of death for many friendships and relationships. I found myself by myself all the time. I had pushed everyone that ever loved me away because I was dead inside. No sign of life, nor any feelings of wanting to live. I gradually stopped going to church. I stopped calling my friends and when they called me to check if I was ok, I wouldn't answer nor return their calls. Until one weekend, I remember sitting on my sofa in my dark living room, watching the television watch me. I heard a voice inside of me saying, "Why are you allowing this to break you? Do you want to die here? Do you want to die in this state you're in? Don't you know there is more for you to see and experience in life? Don't you know that your children are watching you fade away? Is this what you want?" With tears welling up in my eyes and falling down my cheeks, I began to weep. I wanted the bitterness and helplessness to go away so desperately that I got up from the sofa, walked towards my bedroom, grabbed a bottle of pills I had from a surgery, opened it and poured about 20 into the palm of my hand. As I stood in the middle of the floor I looked up and saw my reflection in the mirror staring back at me. "God why? Why was I the one who had to go through this? I finally found someone who cherished and accepted me, who loved me unconditionally, but you took him from me. There isn't anything for me to live for." At that point, I remember a still small voice beyond my cries. It spoke to me saying, "I singled you out to break the curse. Trust Me and Live."

I laid on the floor and cried for hours fighting for my life. I was at war with my thoughts and emotions. That night I asked God if I lived, please reveal to me why He chose me. As I laid there in the middle of my bedroom in a puddle of my tears, I knew there was more to my story than to allow my children to find me dead. Leaving them with the generational curse of suicide passed down from my mother, to me, and now to them. That was the moment I made a decision to use my voice. At that point in my grief process it all was unfolding and developing me into becoming a conduit to ameliorate and liberate others from the bondage of oppression, depression, grief, hopelessness, and doubt. I was charged with standing for those who are in a war battling between life and death. In that moment, I made the choice to be bold, strong, and immovable. In the chaos and pain, I became sober in thought and strategic in movement. I began to embody those attributes of a woman who had found her voice. The woman who finds her voice, is a woman also finds favor with God and man. She is convinced that whatever she puts her hands to do she will complete with excellence. This woman knows that she has a purpose, and there is nothing that is going to stop her from completing it. She is a woman of integrity, character, dignity, grace and pride. She is humble in all that she does. She knows when she speaks, people will listen. This is the woman that knows the power of her voice. This is who I am. This is who you are destined to be.

Once I found my voice, I made a conscious decision to use it to empower women of all ages, social, economic, and spiritual backgrounds. I am here to support you on your journey of discovering your worth, ambitions, and passions in order to become the best version of yourself. I believe my voice is a tool to awaken the greatness that has been lying dormant for far too long. Finally, I decided to use my platform to help revive the broken places of your heart, your home, your dreams, and your visions. My desire is that my voice brings hope and faith back into the grief-stricken. My vision is to Help, Empower, and Rebuild women to discover H.E.R Vision™.

Understanding the power of your voice is understanding the power in the words you speak. Our voices have the power to build up or tear down, to motivate or discourage. It has the power to heal or hurt. While exploring the power of my voice, I've learned that the power isn't so much about what words are spoken, but more so about who is speaking. The power lies in who carries the words. What you have experienced is packed with power. The mere fact that you have overcome those experiences and made it out to the other side to tell the story- that's where the power lies. My words, as a widow, are impactful not only because of what I speak but because I have experienced the pain. The lonely nights of hugging the sheets wishing my deceased husband was there. My prayer is that my story touches the breastplate of your pain to produce the healing power and divine moment for your testimony of how you overcame your pain. I have walked this road; I have felt the impact of its devastation firsthand.

I have come to understand the power of the words in this book. God sets us up in peculiar seasons in our lives that pushes us to purpose. Although those seasons are sometimes very painful, I believe that what we do with that pain defines our purpose. We can decide to sit back and die in our pain, or we can go from pain to power. The bible tells us we overcome by the blood of the lamb and the word of our testimony. We don't only overcome the situation, we overcome the pain of that season. God sets us up so we can tell our testimonies to free others. He created us to be carriers of purpose and power. The power that our voice carries breaks the chains of bondage to those that are bound. It devours and dismantles the plans and schemes of our adversaries. It is important for us to know and understand how many lives(women, men, hurting people, those who have lost hope) depend on our words. When we speak, our words are sent on assignment. Our experiences also have an assignment. The journey isn't ideal, it surely isn't something we have asked for, but we must understand that there are lessons and purpose attached to it. We won't ever walk away empty handed.

Introduction

I am a woman that has faced many disappointments in my life, this was just another one to add to my list. The loss of my husband not only altered the direction of my life, but had forced me into a place of the unknown. The days ahead were intense and very reflective. I'd asked myself repeatedly, "What's out there for me now?" "Where do I go from here?" "How do I survive with only half of me?" "Do I still have a purpose now that I am widowed?" The lack of clarity was overwhelming as I became blinded by a slew of unanswered questions and confusion. I confidently fulfilled my role as a wife. I knew how to fulfill my role as mother and even knew how to minister to the world at large. But widowhood wasn't something I signed up for. I didn't have the slightest idea of how to live this role. I was lost, abandoned, and confused. I had no idea what the next steps were for myself, my children, or my future. One thing I did know, I had lost the love of my life and he wasn't coming back. With each moment, I sunk deeper and deeper into hopelessness with words that echoed in my abandoned heart "He was stripped away by death…now what?"

What I've learned through my loss is that God sets us up in peculiar seasons in our lives that pushes us to purpose. Although those seasons are sometimes very painful, I believe that what we do with that pain defines who we are. We can decide to sit back and die or we can go from pain to power. The bible tells us that we are overcome by the blood of the lamb and the word of our testimony. We don't only overcome the situation, we overcome the pain of that particular season. God sets us up so we can use our voice and tell our testimonies to free others. God made us carriers of purpose and power. We have the power to break chains of bondage in those that are bound. It devours and dismantles the plans and schemes of our adversaries. It is important for us to know and understand how many lives (women, men, hurt people, those who have lost hope) depend on our words. When we speak, our words are sent on assignment. Our experiences also have an assignment. The journey isn't ideal, it surely isn't something we have asked for, but we must understand that there are lessons attached to it. We won't ever walk away empty handed.

The purpose of this book is to revive the hearts of those who've lost loved ones. Losing someone is the hardest thing a person can ever go through. I wouldn't wish this pain on my worst enemy. In my case it was my husband, but for you it could've been a child, a mother, father, grandparent, or sibling. The book may not apply to you at this moment, but it may be fitting for another season of your life or perhaps it is for someone you know. One thing I learned is grief is a road everyone has to travel at some point in their natural life. The upside is, not everyone has to suffer the way I did. Completing this book was truly one of the hardest things I've ever had to do besides burying my husband. It was also one of the most important things I've ever had to do besides getting out of my bed of depression and deciding to live again. My family, future, and ministry depended on it. If my story does anything for anyone, my desire is that the experiences I've written about help you in your process of healing so that you, too, can live again. My prayer is that the tools in this book help make your journey just a little easier by releasing you from the cycle of grief that has kept you bound. I am confident that if you remain faithful to the process, take the tools that are given to you, and apply them to your life; you will not only be on your way to your winning season but to your Winning Lifestyle™. Living while grieving has not always been easy, but worth it. The many people that were and still remain in my corner, pushing me to complete this assignment, have given me the courage to tell my story. I hope it encourages you to tell yours.

Wounded

Desiring someone to notice the pain that was tormenting me beyond the smile they saw on my face has always been a struggle for me. I was the person who no one would ever know what I was privately dealing with. Over the years, I've learned to disguise my pain with a smile. I was the master of masking my issues. From a young girl I faced a roller coaster of emotions. I've never really been the type that was openly expressive regarding my feelings or what I've dealt with. The scars I suffered in silence made me numb to the reality of ever believing my suffering would be heard.

Allow me the opportunity to share a small, but intricate part of my early childhood, the beginning of my journey of silent suffering. I am the only girl of three siblings. Oftentimes, I felt like a target for boys and men who came around. Already consumed with abandonment by my parents and struggling with rejection from who I considered family, I was overwhelmed by being in an environment where I felt out of place. What was a young girl to do other than fight to survive?

My biological mother left my father when I was only two years old. My father left my brothers and I in the care of my grand aunt who had no biological children of her own. Many times, I remember asking her to tell me about my biological mother. My grand aunt would tell me that she wasn't in agreement with the way my father treated my mother. She told me she loved my mother very much. My father on the other hand, not so much. My mother's name was Crystal. From what I was told, she was an amazing woman. She was tall with long fiery red hair. Her frame was thick and beautiful. She had freckles all over her face that went down her neck to the rest of her body. Her personality was one of a black woman in a white woman's body. One that was bold, confident, and sure in her love for her children and her husband. Her love was attached to protection like a lioness and her cubs. I never understood what that meant until I got older. My grand aunt would tell me stories of how she acted so country and was very loud. Most importantly, I was told that she undeniably loved her four children. That statement will forever remain sealed in my heart.

Naturally, it was very difficult to deny the heart wrenching thought over and over, year after year, "If she loved me so much, how could she leave me?" It was a question that reminded me that I was a motherless, abandoned, rejected little girl who desired love from her mother which she would never receive. How could I ever come to terms with this? Never hearing her voice, never feeling her touch, not a hug or a kiss on the forehead. That took a toll on me growing up. Seeing my friends with their mothers, being able to express the love they shared with their mothers was something I longed for. A desire I could never fulfill.

When I was eight I remember asking my grand-aunt if it would be ok to call her mommy – her response was You can call me what you want From that moment, she became my mother. She was very compassionate and generous when it came to opening her doors to people in the neighborhood, her friends and family. After all, she had opened her home to my brothers and I, extending love and compassion to us as children who were in the foster care system. She was the type of person who would feed the hungry, clothe the shirtless, and house the homeless without second thought. I admired her for that- a true Christian woman.

I remember being about nine years old when she allowed my cousin who was recently released from prison to come live with us while he worked on rebuilding his life on the outside. When he first came home it was fun, he'd take my brothers and I to the park, feed us, take us to school in the mornings and pick us up at dismissal. He gained our trust. One day I got in trouble in school, and they called home. My mother was extremely upset because she never had any problems out of me regarding school. So, she told my cousin about the incident, and he assured her saying, "Don't worry I will discipline her for you." I was in complete shock that she would agree to him disciplining me, especially because I was so young at the time. I didn't understand why he would volunteer to do such a thing.

I was terrified. I will never forget the smirk on his face as he took me into my mother's room and told me to be very quiet. He then revealed his secret, he hadn't planned on beating me at all. In fact, His plan was to pretend by slamming his hand on the bed. All I had to do was scream every time his hand struck the bed to make it seem like he

22

was disciplining me. I looked at him with a sigh of relief... and confusion. Naively enough, at this point I was totally confident that he had my back. I felt a sense of protection, especially with the lack of a father figure. I thought the plan was quite brilliant and amusing but I was not aware that he was setting the stage for a vicious scheme.

Saturday mornings were the best mornings in my house as a child. My brothers and I would wake up to a nice hot breakfast then watch cartoons until we'd fall asleep late into the afternoon. Well, this was while my great uncle was alive. My mother was married to the best man ever. The day I asked my mother if I could call her Mommy was the day I made my great-uncle a very happy man. I became his little girl. He took such great care of my brothers and i. He cooked, he cleaned, took us to school, and picked us up most days. I remember he would walk me to the store for candy. Oh yes! Mike's candy store was the best store in Bushwick, Brooklyn for children. He was the first real father figure in my life. I looked past his struggles with alcohol because he was the man I looked up to as a young girl. He was my example of how a man should treat a lady.

This particular Saturday morning I decided to sleep late. I was awakened by the laughter of my brothers playing in my mother's bedroom. My mother called out for me. I guess she wanted to know if I was still sleeping. I heard her but did not move because I just wanted to lay there and do nothing, just as I had done so many Saturdays before. When I didn't hear her voice any longer, I heard footsteps coming towards my room. I yelled, "Mommy is that you?" and suddenly a silhouette appeared in the doorway. It was my cousin. I thought to myself, "Why is he walking so quietly?". I knew something wasn't right by the look in his eyes. I asked what he was doing in my room and without answering he turned his back to me. I thought he was going to leave but instead he closed himself in. He then bolted towards me and grabbed me so fast that I didn't have enough time to scream. He held my body down and put his hands over my mouth. I couldn't breathe. Tears rolled down my face as he forced himself inside of me. I just laid there completely numb and shocked. All that went through my head was how desperately I wanted my daddy. I needed someone to step in and protect me. But no one was there to rescue my nine-year-old body from being ravaged by the man I trusted to care for me. I couldn't escape the scent of his vanilla cologne that filled the room. It turned my stomach and seemed to stick to me even after he finally removed himself from being on top of me. I'm not sure how long it lasted, but it felt like forever. With one hand over my mouth and the other on my leg he had positioned himself perfectly for animalistic thrusts into my nine-year-old body. He panted. Huffing and hovering over me while saying, "I knew you wanted this. You ain't no little girl, you grew up now. You're mine now!" The more he spoke, the more I fought. The more I fought, the more forceful he became. Not knowing what else to do I remained still, lifeless, crying until he had finally stopped. As he stood, he stared intensely into my eyes and pointed his finger in my face. "If you tell anyone, I will kill you. Even if you tell, no one will believe you anyway because you're a fast little girl." He left the room as abruptly as he came in and went on with the day as if it were just another Saturday afternoon. But for me, it would be the first Saturday that I would yearn for the innocent weekends of old. While he was able to return to life as usual and everyone played and laughed and cooked, I would never be the same again. I was scared. I was scarred.

I was confused. Did I somehow deserve this? Was he disciplining me for some wrongdoing I knew nothing about? Had I sent a message to him that this is what I wanted? Did my mother agree to this? I had no answers or insight. There was no comfort, only chaos. I was more alone than I had ever been. Not knowing what else to do, I immediately got up and went to the tub as quickly and quietly as I could. I wanted to yell out to my mother, but I was afraid that he would hear me calling out to her and come quickly to silence my cries before she could hear me. So, I wept alone crouched in the corner of the tub. Before long, my mother appeared. Should I tell her what just happened? What if she wouldn't believe me? I stayed silent. A wave of anger came over me. Looking at her enraged me. Where was my protection? How did you not see this coming? Or did you care at all if it did? Perhaps this was another way to penalize me for being different, for being lighter skinned. Or maybe she didn't anticipate this at all and could've helped me if I would've just told her what had just happened. It was too late. I had already been ruined. The damage was done. "I want my real mother!", I exclaimed with my quivering prepubescent voice. Perceived as being disrespectful, I was scolded. Told me to stop crying, go to my room and get dressed before my brothers came into the room. My brothers?! They were the least of my worries when there was a monster in our home. And she was the one who invited him in. She always welcomed everyone in. All she knew was that she was doing the Lord's work.

My surrogate mother, Hazel Goode, was a woman of faith. She never bore any children. I assume that when four children showed up at her door, she was more than happy to take the opportunity that knocked. I cannot deny that she loved us. She just didn't have the tools to care for four children who had trauma at such a young age. But she did her best. She made sure we had "quality clothes" according to her sense of fashion. I mean, at age eleven and twelve none of my peers at my school appreciated Liz Claiborne or Jones New York. Only the teachers knew what those labels were. Outside of that, she fed us, took us to the doctor, and always made sure we were at our weekly visit to see our father. She was a great provider. She even sent us to the best private schools. She had to wake us up early and we had to be dressed by 7am. The drive was halfway across town but that did not stop her from dropping us off and picking us up on time every single day. I must say, in hindsight, that I didn't have a bad childhood especially considering that if she hadn't taken me in, I would be living with strangers. Many nights I asked myself, would I have been better off with strangers?

She had an angry streak though. I remember times when I was around twelve years old that she would get mad and would drag me by the hair across the floor. Yelling as she paced, "You think you are better than me because you're a little white ass? Well, you're not. You're not better than me. I will show you." I could not understand her means of punishment. Her methods seemed so extreme compared to the things I was accused of. I was such a timid child, so playful and innocent. At that age I was still playing with dolls. How, then, is being dragged across the floor appropriate for not sweeping the floor or forgetting to take out the garbage? I wasn't disobedient or mischievous like my brothers who were living a street life. It appears I had become her punching bag when she was angry with them but couldn't control them. Once again, the person I loved, trusted, and thought would protect me was the very person who was abusing me. Through all of that I loved her still.

Although she never told us that she loved us, there were so many ways she showed it. I now understand that her love language was Acts of service; she expressed her love by doing things for us. For so long, I still just wanted to hear her say it. I wanted so badly to hear it from her because I knew I would never hear them from my natural mother.

There were so many things I left unsaid. I never expressed my requests for loving words and never verbalized my disappointments or pain. I never told anyone the secret of what happened to me in my room that Saturday or any of the many other times I was preyed on as a child. I didn't have the courage to mumble a word because I always felt rejected by my family. I was afraid to be viewed as a liar or attention seeker. I packed away these secrets for more than half of my life. I buried my hurt behind walls of anger, rejection, abandonment, and self-sabotage. That secrecy fed cycles of lack of trust, resentment and hate which took root and almost destroyed my very existence. It grew from isolation to rebelliousness and then back into a shell throughout my adolescence. I didn't have many friends and my brothers had chosen the streets so I had grown in the understanding that the only person who could protect me was me.

Journaling became my go-to. Writing distracted me from the suffering and pain of my childhood that no one knew about. It was my therapeutic outlet that allowed me to express myself, while my wounds remained undisclosed to those around me. I learned that we must confront our pain before it consumes us. I had finally found a way to release all that I had suffered in silence, and I began to treat the scars no one had seen.

Silent Scars

Scars are always a representation of endured pain. The healthy healing process of a scar is treatment from a doctor. Your doctor will give you an ointment or antibiotic depending on the severity of your scar. Oftentimes, when treated properly the scar will heal from the inside out with the application of the doctor's instructions. If the scar goes untreated over time, it eventually becomes infected and can worsen far beyond the initial pain that was inflicted. Sometimes that pain comes from the nerves that develop after the injury which appear to be healed on the outside but remain damaged internally. The wound eventually has the ability to affect other parts of the body outside of the directly injured area. This leads to subsequent pain, which can mean the scarred tissue has taken the place of the healthy tissue. As time passes and the scar goes untreated, in addition to the increasing pain you may also experience lack of function in the affected area along with the surrounding areas.

The process of correction to scars is vast. Some may need topical solutions and others may need a technique called Dermabrasion that requires multiple sessions over a period of time. Doctors say the downside to this, is it will make the affected area appear more noticeable. However, it goes away over time with necessary continuous treatment. Topical treatments are for minor scars that had begun treatment but was terminated prematurely. Why am I explaining scars and treatment? My research about scars, their ability to affect healthy nerves and the different treatments depending on the severity of the wound, was revelatory to me. It revealed that for so many years I walked around with scars I couldn't identify and hadn't treated. The depth of some of my scars, I believe, damaged other healthy areas in my life. In hindsight, I can now see that I obtained many of my scars from childhood. They were never appropriately addressed and as a result they became infected. It is imperative that the scars from our childhood are treated properly at conception in order to ensure the appropriate treatment for our total healing. There are no topical treatments that can help the depth of some of our pain. We can attempt to heal in isolation or treat our wounds by talking to friends, but our scars that live beneath the surface exist beyond the reach of any person. The infected areas of our hearts need a Godly surgical treatment that only the Father can perform.

Suffering in silence many times can be the result of childhood history of physiological and emotional effects from abuse, abandonment, or rejection. Abandonment can stem from a loss of a loved one or someone leaving your life unexpectedly. It can also stem from lack of emotional and physical care as a child. When these issues aren't addressed in childhood, that child grows into an adult and perpetuates the cycle of abandonment which may have been passed down from generation to generation. This in turn creates what most might know as self-sabotage due to the fear of being rejected, abandoned or abused by those closest to them or those who might get close. Self-sabotage first begins in a person's mind with faulty thought processes about how you think about people, your relationships with people, and your expectations of how it will turn out. Predictions such as the thought of a person leaving or facing difficult situations may prompt triggers of the feeling of abuse, rejection and self-worthlessness that was never addressed from the past. The actions and feelings mentioned are sure signs of someone who is approaching or currently on the road to self-sabotage.

I remember a period where I experienced extreme depression. I'd just gone through a horrible break up. The way I felt about this person was very similar to the way I felt about my deceased husband. I never thought I would be able to feel that way again, but he came and swept me off my feet. I mean, he would tell me things like "I see you; I see your pain and I will never drop you." and "You are amazing. From the moment I saw you I knew you were the one for me." Now, initially I was over the moon and wanted nothing more but for this relationship to stand the test of time. I remember having a conversation with Jesus one night, saying to the Lord, "I want to be healed for this relationship to succeed." As time went on, I quickly realized that I could not desire to be healed and whole solely for the sake of a relationship. My desire to be healed should have been for me first. If you aren't yet healed and don't know what it is to be whole by yourself, then you aren't ready to be in a relationship with anyone else. The second most important relationship anyone can have is with themselves! The first one is with the Father in heaven.

As that relationship grew - I would've loved to say it grew stronger but unfortunately it didn't because I began to self sabotage. I am by no means saying the demise of the relationship was all on me. What I am saying is the more he reassured me that he loved me, the more skeptical I became of his sincerity. He tried his best to show me that I was the only one for him. We prayed together, we ministered together, we even took family trips together. We traveled all over the world and nothing was ever good enough for him to prove himself to me. Through all of that, we never stood a chance. I pushed him away before he could ever truly get close. I questioned the relationship and felt like it was too good to be true. My thought process was "He's lying, he could never be with just me." or "He will leave eventually." Well, that's exactly what happened, the relationship came to an end. I know I broke his heart the day he walked out of my house. I told him I was done, and it was over between us. Something was different that night, I had attempted to push him away before, but I'd never said those words to him. We'd argue like any other couple, but this time was drastically different. For almost two years I suppose I'd always had those words reserved in my heart but never mustered up enough courage to say them until then. That night, I succumbed to my fear of rejection and the cycle of self-sabotage prevailed. I was so in love with him; I felt safe with him, I felt like someone actually saw me for me and the pain that came along with it. He took time with me, we cried together, I was able to talk about my deceased husband freely with no judgment. I believe we could have been something great if I would not have allowed fear to control me. I will never forget the look in his eyes the night he walked out of my house. I cried until the sun came up because I knew I could have given more of myself, but the fear of being crushed by love, and the thought that at some point he would've walked out on me would not allow me to commit. I couldn't stop my feelings of not being good enough for him. I self-sabotaged that relationship hands down. As time went on, I fell deeper and deeper into a depression. It deepened the already existing wounds of isolation and rejection that I struggled with for so long. I cried everyday. I laid on the sofa day in and day out having no desire to do anything, go anywhere, or even speak to anyone. My children at this point were a bit older and my goddaughter was living with me, so I felt like I didn't have to mother anyone. Honestly, I didn't have the energy to do that anyway. Once again, I found myself alone in a state of being rejected and abandoned- even though I caused it. Even though I knew I had a part to play in it, I couldn't shake the feeling that I was dropped again by someone who said they wouldn't ever leave. The silent scars of my past ran deep. They were not visible for the natural eye to see, but the scars definitely affected the surrounding healthy tissue which were trust, self-worth, and acceptance.

Healed, So I Thought

That failed relationship changed me forever. After finding myself in that familiar place of abandonment, neglect, and rejection when he walked out that door, I remember waking up after many nights of overwhelming sorrow saying to myself "I want out of this cycle!" I didn't want to feel that pain even for one more moment. I got up from my bed and called my insurance company to find a therapist. Now I know this is taboo for the 'Saints of God'. Most of us have been taught that if we go to God in prayer, we will find every answer. That message underhandedly reinforced that there wasn't a need to seek answers on someone's couch. But I knew I needed something more after I got off my knees from prayer. I wanted to be healthy and whole! Not just healed but be healthy mentally, spiritually, and emotionally. I knew I would feel rejection and abandonment in life again, but I wanted the posture of my response to change.

I believe when we change our posture towards what we feel in the moment, then our response towards our situations will reap a different result. Whenever I felt rejected or abandoned, I went into a deep depression. I didn't have the skill set to articulate my feelings. Growing up, my mother wasn't raised to express her feelings, nor did she ever develop the skill set to pass onto me. My mother was raised in an era where parents didn't talk about feelings with their children. In my mother's era, the priority was staying alive. Feelings didn't put food on the table nor clothes on your back, so it was not deemed as something worth prioritizing. My mother was caring, but the expression of feelings didn't exist. Not because she didn't want to connect but because she didn't know how. Therefore, I wasn't fully equipped to deal with life's challenges. Truth be told, you too may have found yourself (or currently find yourself) in that same predicament. For this reason, I believe this section will not only help you, but I pray it encourages you to seek professional help, outside of your pastors or spiritual leaders.

I knew I needed to seek professional counsel when, day after day, I didn't have enough, nor did I want to find the energy to get out of bed. Then there were times I would go on with life as usual outwardly but felt like I was dying inside. I would weep some mornings as I opened my eyes because God woke me up. I wanted so desperately for Him to put me and my misery to rest. I wanted the pain to disappear and never return. The best way to have the pain lift would be for life to end. So, I went to my cabinet and took out a bottle of pills while my children weren't home. They had simply thought all this time that mommy wasn't feeling good. I wasn't feeling good! I was in anguish and needed relief from the wounds that no one could see. I took a handful of Advil that day and went to sleep. I remember waking up and crying like a baby, "Lord Why did you allow me to wake up? Why are you keeping me here?" Those questions continued to rule my mind space for years. Angry, sad, and depressed. I felt all these things so deeply, so persistently. Yet, no one saw "Me"! I expressly wanted someone to see past this masked smile and see my anguish.

This was the pivotal point in my life. I aspired to be different. I thirsted to see a new Vioree. I was hungry to experience something different in my life. One where the cycles of sorrow and fear would be broken. Most of all, I longed for the understanding of the root to my pain, and I was finally ready to refuse to engage in self-sabotaging behavior ever again. I started seeing a therapist. My readiness for change allowed me to remain dedicated to the process. My sessions were 7am in Manhattan; I traveled from Brooklyn into the city early each morning because I wanted to prove to myself how hungry I was for change. We started the sessions with "Why are you here?" I replied, "Where do I start?". That broke the ice. I shared everything with her about the breakup, losing my husband, being homeless, being a battered wife with two small children, being raped, my mother leaving and committing suicide when I was nine years old. I mean I laid it on her thick. She listened week after week, and I kept going back. I remained determined and vulnerable so that I could successfully unpack my past.

Then we got to the topic of my childhood. I sat on her couch and cried like a baby. I remember her telling me, "If you don't get it out through tears and talking it will come out through anger and decisions you won't be proud of." That was the moment I began to spill the beans which, I believe, was one of the best decisions I've ever made for myself. Many people believe that talking to someone is taboo and that anyone willing to do so should be labeled as

41

crazy. This isn't the case at all... it is simply admitting that you aren't perfect. Therapy is liberating because you can speak to someone about all that is going on inside of you without judgment or shame. When you actively take steps toward your healing, you can start your process of wholeness.

Widowed

I'd gotten to a place where I thought I'd overcome the tears. Then, through every fading minute and every passing thought there they came streaming down again. That day continually replayed in my head. That moment – a thought wrecking echo – when the doctor came out of the room where his body laid. The look in her eyes as she walked towards me. My heart dropped; I knew there were words to follow the blank stare on her face. I couldn't fathom the idea of her saying anything other than he's going to be ok. That was my moment of a hoop dream, live and in color. As she continued to walk towards me, I felt my body fading from me. I knew something wasn't right, as she got closer and closer, it felt like I was further and further away from the happy ending I'd desired. Then, at that moment "Sorry Mrs. Brandon" I'll never forget the look in her eyes, the touch of her hand sliding down my arm; my life with him flashed before me all in a split second. I couldn't breathe – the feeling like a python was clinched around my neck, choking the life out of me. Flashes of our friendship, our

43

first kiss, our home together, raising our children; the day he told me he loved me, our first meal, the one he made for me. The feeling of life was leaving my body. I began to fall. The thoughts of everything we built slowly drifted away. All that was left was the memories of him unbeknownst to me, his legacy was just beginning.

How was I going to tell my children that their father wasn't coming home anymore? Thoughts raced through my head of the pain that they were going to feel. the anger that may consume their little hearts. Maybe I was overthinking this. To some of his family members my children were just my children, not taking into consideration the man my husband was. Jaida was only two years old when I met Nathaniel, John was six. I worked as a dance teacher for an after-school program called Guardian Angels in Brooklyn NY. Nathaniel, known by many as "Chee-Chee" and known by many musicians as "The Maestro" (He was just that good in his day.) Chee-Chee was also an instructor at the same after school program. I brought John to work with me one day and sent him into the gym where Chee-Chee was playing basketball with the children. I was a little apprehensive at first, but my supervisor at the time reassured me that John would be ok with Chee-Chee. So, I went on to teach my dance class. After work that day we were introduced by our supervisor who later would become my pastor. I was engaged at the time of our meeting. Chee-Chee and I became friends, well we did see each other almost every day because of work. I did not know he was the musician for our supervisor's church which was directly across the street from where I went to church. Our churches began fellowshipping together, I began teaching the dancers at my supervisor's church which meant we saw each other more and more. My finances at the time, and I got into a huge altercation which resulted in violence. Let's just say he will never put his hands on another woman as long as he lives. He absolutely has a scar above his eye to remind him. Needless to say, we separated which in hindsight was the best day of Chee-Chee and my life. Chee-Chee was there for me as a friend the entire time of my healing and transition process. He was hilarious, always kept me laughing to get my mind off the legal trouble I was facing. He always made sure I ate which for those that know me know that is one of my soft spots. I remember him telling me after we were married that he would go up to Harlem and buy me these Philly Cheesesteak sandwiches that I loved just to see me smile. He lived in Brooklyn, so he would take a two-hour ride on the train before work to pick up a sandwich for me. He always went the extra mile to ensure I was happy. I trusted him, by this time I'd landed a government job and needed someone to pick up the children for me after school. Well, I did not look far, he was right there to help me with them. When I got home, Jaida was fed and bathed. John's homework was done, and they watched television waiting for me. I thought it was all too good to be true. Jaida and Chee-Chee had the most beautiful bond, one which she lacked with her biological father, which set my heart ablaze for him. I never thought there would be a man out there that would not only love me but love my children that were not his own but there he was, appearing in the toughest time in my life. After coming out of two abusive relationships, to have a man come along and be so patient with me, who cooked, cleaned, and loved my children felt like a dream come true. He became my best friend, easy to talk to, kind and gentle when it came to the kids and me. Not once did he make advances at me, he genuinely desired to be my friend.

He was an old fashion type of guy. I remember the first time he asked me out on a date. It was a Wednesday afternoon, while sitting around the cafeteria with other co-workers, he was being a jokester as he always was. One of the co-workers asked him to take the kids outside, and he responded with "Sure, only if Vioree goes out with me." I laughed because he was always joking about something. But it seemed like I was the only one that caught the joke, because I was left laughing by myself. I was unaware he'd expressed his interest in me to our supervisor and coworkers but never directly told me. He looked over at me and said in front of everyone, "Vioree, can I take you to eat?" Now he knew I wasn't going to say no to food, so I replied with "Sure, you know I love a good meal." From that day on, we were inseparable, spending every day together. Were we the real-life Frick and Frack.

I remember one day he was cooking in my kitchen, while I was sitting watching television. John and Jaida went to their grandmother's house. He said, Vioree, you want to be my wife? I said "Huh". He said "come here" I got up, walked towards the kitchen, looked at him as he said "You wanna be my wife?" I said, sure why not. Very informal, but the most romantic thing I ever experienced in my life. We were married within three weeks. Yes, it was fast but, when a man knows he knows. Jaida and John gained a father, and I gained an entire family. His family treated us as though we were a part of their family for years. Well, that goes for some of his family. Things weren't perfect but they were all worth it, every struggle, every argument, every tear shed. I had the honor of doing it with the love of my life.

Driving home from the hospital everything was going through my head, how was I going to tell my children that the only father that they really knew was gone. To Jaida, Chee-Chee was daddy, to John, he was the man that taught him how to be himself, he was the man that showed him how his mother was supposed to be treated, without the abuse, without the shouting or hitting. I didn't feel strong enough to utter those words to them because not only did the thought break me, but I also knew it would break them when those words hit the portal of their ears, going through the canal and piercing their souls. I wasn't ready for that, but I knew it had to be done. I was now approaching the corner of my block; tears began to trickle down my face and I walked in and saw my babies sitting on the floor so innocently. I remember John, looking into his tender eyes, and him saying Mommy, he isn't coming home, is he? I remember saying no baby, Jaida barely could talk, and Camille (our baby girl) was only two years old, looking at me for answers. I said to them, "Chee-Chee went to heaven, He is with Jesus and the angels". John began to cry uncontrollably, Jaida said I want daddy to come home mommy, Camille, not really understanding why John and Jaida were crying, also began to cry. I sat in the middle of the living room floor and cried as I held my babies. unable to really understand the pain that they were feeling as children, all I knew was I became a broken wounded woman again. Left to pick up the pieces as a single mother with three babies. I wanted my husband, and I wanted my children to have their dad back.

Days and nights – even months at a time I didn't understand why God would take the rock of our family. Of course, the only person I could blame was God himself. The questions of "why" flooded my mind. My thoughts consumed my very existence. Why did God take my best friend? My precious jewel. This felt very personal! He was loved by so many, but for me, he was my husband, the closest person to me. The only one I trusted with my life. I thought to myself what made God so upset with me that He would take a husband from his wife, a Father from his children, a son from his mother, a brother from his sister? Why would He shatter a family that was bound together in love, happiness and most of all the presence of each other which made our world complete. It felt like the wrath of God was prevalent towards me and my family. "Why?" was the important question. I cried myself to sleep trying to figure out why God would do this to me!

I remember one night placing my husband's shirt on the side of the bed where he slept and laying on top of it. The smell of his cologne was fresh. He enjoyed getting dressed really nice and spraying himself down with some sweet-smelling colognes. He loved Dolce & Gabbana light blue. I woke up several times that night in puddles of my tears. The smell of him consumed my nostrils, what was worse was the thought of never feeling him again. In my mind I expected him to walk through the door at any moment from a hard day's work. That minute turned into hours, those hours turned into days, then days turned into months, now months into years. Brokenness was an understatement to explain the state I was in. I knew in my heart God was in charge and He loved me, but in that moment, I did not feel His love. How could a gentle, loving, compassionate, healing God inflict this much pain on me?

Having a conversation with God one night; I asked Him "Did I not give you enough? I preached your word, danced before you with all my might, my heart is pure towards you. My children serve you; I am a wife that loved her husband and he loved me. So why?! Why would you impose so much grief onto me? My soul screamed why! {"Would you crush my heart with a pain that cannot be uttered?"} Sounds crazy huh! Whelp, that was me, angry as hell! Many people say we aren't supposed to question God, but I had questions and lots of them. I wanted answers and I wanted them right then. I wasn't concerned with the consequences of my questions. There is much to be said about questioning His decisions, or even asking "WHY?". I've realized those are the moments when the Real you has to face a Real God. The question of why isn't a question of doom, it is one that breaks up the ground where the core of your torment is rooted. It is a process for all of us as believers to trust by eliminating the "Why?" factor. The

"Why?'' factor is what I call a series of questions when faced with incomprehensible situations– leading up to God's Divine Purpose for your life. My revelation of the why factor consists of a series of events which takes place in our lives that sets in motion the formula for discovering our life's purpose. For every stage of our lives, we must face something that challenges our faith. Every one of us will get to a place or have been in a place in life where we have found ourselves asking God "WHY?". If you haven't experienced that yet – as my mother would say "Chile keep on living". When we ask why it sets in motion a series of questions such as Why am here? Why did you choose me? Why have I experienced so many twists and turns in my life? Why won't things change for me? Asking why is necessary and makes you human. When we ask the question, it allows us to process the loss and reinvest energy into our healing; it releases us from the ties of our pain and creates the space to remember with joy instead of anger, resentment, and confusion. The "Why?" factor is the desire to find answers for your current state and for your future. Finally, it allows us to grieve unapologetically. It does not convict you of your feelings, it is simply designed to take you beyond your comfort zone, strengthen your faith and bring you to a place of acceptance and live a prosperous life without your loss.

As I recap the past ten years of my life, from this point. I realized that I was facing another episode of "disappointment". I found myself wounded from my past, and now widowed involuntarily. The rage that consumed my very existence was unfathomable. I knew that I was in a danger zone when I found myself angry about everything.

Displaced

For a long time, I didn't want to accept or even acknowledge I was a widow. I couldn't utter the word. When it was time for me to complete legal documents following Chee-Chee's passing, I would cry every time I looked at the section where they ask Single, Married, Divorced, Widowed. I was in total denial, angry that I was even in this situation, and depressed not realizing I was going through according to the Kubler Ross theory – Five Stages of Grief. What baffled me is that no one around me identified with my grief nor could speak to those areas of it.

The moment I realized I was a widow–it hit me like a ton of bricks. This marital status was looked at in society as a color – dark! When people think of a widow they immediately think of sadness, grief, loneliness, poverty, anger, and survival. I guess no one gets married thinking they will lose their spouse. For a long time, I did everything on my own. When I met my husband, I was a single mother raising two children. I divorced my children's father because of domestic abuse. One thing I've learned, the process of divorce feels equivalent to death. Grieving what could have been, the desire of what you wanted, and the reality of what was. That is exactly what it feels like when you lose a spouse. Coming out of an abusive relationship with my ex-husband of six years was traumatizing for not only myself but also for my children. I was playing the cards I'd been dealt – which was to be the best single mother I could, considering I had no road map to a successful home environment. Dealing with the abandonment and abuse of that relationship feeling worthless, put me in survival mode. I always had a sense of resilience. Always one to pick myself up and keep moving forward. Having children heightened that trait in me all the more, because I not only had to do it for me, but I also now had children that relied on me. Being in an abusive relationship with my ex-husband brought back memories of my childhood.

My father was abusive to my mother. I remember a time my mother and father were arguing in the hallway of our home – he slapped her in front of my brothers and me. I was only about two years old, but I would never forget when she fell to the floor, she looked up at me. I remember the look in her eyes. She was embarrassed, ashamed, and angry, but all she did was lay there and cried. I remember just looking at her with no emotions. Yes, I was only two but that was the last time I ever really remember seeing her. My last memory of her was being slapped by my father across her face. I thought about that moment so many times as I grew up as an adolescent and now as an adult. I wondered why she didn't fight back. Why didn't she o show me that isn't how a man is supposed to treat you? Where was her resilience to survive? Where was her sense of self-worth – enough to show me that she deserved more or that's not what love looks like. The young girl in me wanted her to fight back like I did – maybe then I would've been able to identify an abuser. I wanted her to talk to me about how she felt when he would hit her and what I could to avoid what she'd been through. I wanted her to do so much more than just lay there helplessly. That moment, as she laid on the floor looking up at me I witnessed the third generation of domestic violence. At the tender age of two I was unknowingly exposed to what I would have to fight against in my future. I knew I did not want to be that woman, nor did I want my daughters to grow up seeing me in a position of embarrassment and worthlessness. I was determined to be better and show my daughter better, and I wanted my daughter to grow up in a home with a man that loved her mother and was the example to what a good man looks like. God blessed me with that. A little over three years later I met that man I prayed for, not knowing that I would be tasked with raising children as a single mother, again. Although I didn't have any idea of what God had in store for me, I knew that whatever it was it had to be big.

When you are a widow woman it is easy to be overlooked. But still able to be regarded. You must set yourself apart from the status quo to let people and the system know that "I will not be overlooked! When the odds are against you - That is the tipping point of your breakthrough. That is the moment you know that you are finding your voice. Finding your voice at the least opportune time is the most powerful moment of your life. Remember there is always an advantage when feeling like you're at a disadvantage - the lessons you learn are priceless. You don't want your voice to make you famous, you want it to be effective!

One of my favorite stories in the bible is 1 Kings 17: 17-16 There was a famine in the land. The people were running out of food and water. There was a prophet named Elijah who God directed to leave the place where he was and to travel to a place called Zarephath which belonged to Sidon. God told Elijah that a widow would provide for him. Now what I find interesting about this story on the offset was that God directed Elijah where to go and who would provide for him, but it does not mention that God spoke to the widow and told her that she would have a visitor, nor that she'd have to serve out of her emptiness. There were many times I'd found myself serving while feeling empty or feeling like I had nothing left to give. But God always sent someone to knock on my door and refill my emptiness.

The story goes on to say when Elijah arrived at the gate of the city, there was a widow gathering sticks. He asked her to bring him a little cup of water and some bread. She replies to Elijah "All I have is a handful of flour and a little oil, and I'm gathering some sticks to take home to make this last meal for my son and then we will die." Now, I asked myself why God directed Elijah to go to this widows house knowing how little she had and He knew that was her last supper. But I come to realize, everything that God does has a plan of purpose connected to it. So, Elijah says to the widow, "Don't fear, do as I asked and make a cake and give me the first piece, then make some for you and your son." The widow did as Elijah asked, she made him the cake and fed him first. Elijah told her what the Lord said concerning her and her son "the bin of flour should not be used up, nor shall the jar of oil run dry until the day the Lord sends rain on the earth" as the Lord said, she never went hungry.

I love this passage of scripture because it showed me that although I wasn't prepared for my financial famine, nor was I prepared to become a widow, God was always right there providing for me and protecting me in the midst of that season and every season thereafter. I want to encourage you; God will never leave you in a desolate place. Noticed Elijah nor God identified this widow by name. They just mentioned her as "widow" which means she was the representation for the nameless. For many years as a young widow, I felt nameless to my family, to my church community, and nameless to myself. But just like this widow, God knows exactly where to meet you in your time of need. He will send people to provide, that don't know your name. He has and will always be the Father to the nameless. Speaking to the nameless women, who are feeling displaced. God has a plan for you. The last thing I want to point out which I think is very relevant was her flesh responded with "This is my Last '' but her faith responded with "I trust you Father" it was through her obedience that the Lord provided for her and her child. It was important that her flesh and her faith were not on the same page. I believe she was looking at it like, this prophet has come into my house to ask for the last meal I was going to prepare for my son and I, but her faith said, if this is a false prophet so be it, but I trust the word of the Lord over this situation. God's plan and purpose for our lives and situations that we may be faced with, won't always make sense in the moment. But our obedience and faithfulness to His word will help us through those hard times and tough situations that may seem like death. You may feel displaced, invaluable, or helpless right now, but keep pushing forward. I assure you when you get those feelings ,that purpose won't let you sleep, and pursuing destiny keeps showing up in your dreams. This is a clear identifier that there is something great waiting on the other side for you. Be the woman that pushes against the system that is working against what you need. The system of poverty and the system of "Being alone (not married") makes you invaluable!

I would be doing this book and every reader a disservice if I did not give insight into what widows go through without the support of her government and church, and how she is displaced from her social class. The modern-day widow in the modern-day world. There is much to be desired when it pertains to ministry towards orphans, but hardly any ministries towards widows and not much intention shown towards making steps to address this displaced class of people. The biblical mandate is to care for widows should be an intentional movement in our churches; considering some of the issues widows experience. Before I get into why it is important for our churches to have a refuge, a safe space, or even a space at all set up for widows and widowers. Let's dig into some fun facts to give you some insight on the numbers. According to the US 2019 Census there are 11.27 million widowed women and 3.48 million widowed men living. It is yet to be counted after the COVID-19 pandemic how many widows and widowers there are living in the US. I am sure the numbers are twice that. According to the United Nations there are approximately 258 million widows around the world, nearly one out of 10 widows live in extreme poverty. That is a massive number in one social class when the marital classes are only four (Single, Married, Widowed, Divorced.) Many times, when we think of widows, we think of women over 60 years of age. The unfortunate truth is, after much in depth research the numbers of young widows continue to grow, but the US Census count is undocumented. So, according to the US Census widows are only counted as widows if they are over the age of 60 and are only entitled to all the benefits the government offers if they are 60 years old and have never remarried. This is largely in part due to the laws that were past January 1, 1940. This was passed under the social security, The Federal Old-Age Survivors Insurance Trust Fund which was established as a separate account in the United States Treasury to hold the amounts accumulated under the Old-age and Survivors Insurance Program. This was passed into law to provide benefits to the surviving spouse through the social security office. This law only benefits the surviving spouse if you are over 60. You can only collect benefits at age 60 if never remarried. For all widows and widowers under the age of 60, 50 if you are disabled, there is no governmental plan set up to provide support to widows younger than 60/50 years of age. Therefore, there is a growing number of widows and widowers that become displaced from their homes and left to pick up the pieces alone. For the young widow or widower with children, they are entitled to what is called survivors benefits for the dependent. This gives assistance to the child under the age of 18. For every dependent child, they are entitled to 75% of the deceased parents' basic social security benefits. This seems like a great benefit for the child. It would be, if the deceased parent put in years of service in the workforce. Let's explore again. If the young widow's husband was 25 years old, keep in mind women are becoming widows much younger over the past 20 years. He's just starting out in the workforce, social security is only giving benefits to the dependent child based on what the father paid into social security. Therefore, if he worked only 5 years, whatever he paid into over those 5 years the child is entitled to 75% of whatever the dollar amount is. That isn't a lot of benefits for the dependent child, and the widow isn't entitled to any benefits because under The Federal Old-Age Survivors Insurance Trust Fund she isn't over 60. This leaves the young widow devastated over the loss of her husband, grieving because she cannot provide or support her children.

This is where I believe the church is a vital part in supporting the widows, especially widows in our local assemblies. My experience with the church and being a leader wasn't the greatest. I pray this section brings light in those dark places in ministries where being or even talking about widows are no longer taboo. As mentioned earlier we are seeing widows younger and younger. I became a widow at the age of 30 when my youngest was only two years old. Being in leadership that took on an entirely new identity. I was now a woman in ministry with no husband, feeling uncovered with three small children to care for. There was no safe space or ministry for me to find refuge that helped me get through this new journey I was on. Many Sundays I sat in the clergy section, serving and bleeding. Feeling alone and displaced because there was no place for me anymore. I could no longer attend the marriage ministry events, because I wasn't married. I felt out of place even thinking of attending the singles events because I wasn't single, I wasn't divorced either, my husband had died. I didn't fit in anywhere in the ministry and there was no emotional support provided to women like me. Then to top things off, my pastor at the time sat me down one day and said, He understood what I was going through, I thought to myself, really how could you, your wife is in the sanctuary; he went on to say I really wasn't considered a widow because I was young, and I had the opportunity to wed again. At that moment I knew I was totally alone, for my pastor, my leader not to see me the way God positioned me, was a huge blow to the defined identity of who I currently was. I was totally broken. I'd lost my husband, my friend, my covering and I thought I could receive sound guidance from my leader ,to be told I wasn't what I knew as my new normal, a Widow, was a blow to my soul. That is the moment I became resentful towards the church and ministry. For many years I sat in leadership broken and felt out of place. Here I was evangelizing telling people about God, and how they could come to this house of worship and find peace, joy, and family, when I didn't believe that myself. I had no peace, I definitely didn't have joy, and family wasn't an option for me. I experienced a lot of hurt in that particular ministry, the main reason, I felt displaced from

God's people who were supposed to do as the bible commands, take care of the widow. I felt unworthy and unaccepted in ministry and as a female preacher because I was now a young woman with no covering of a husband or her spiritual Father. I felt hopeless because my husband was the breadwinner for the majority of the income. I thought to myself, how was I going to service with no help from any direction? I did not have family to support me or my children. I was in a true desolate place. These are some of the issues widows young and old deal with. Now, for my bible scholars, I know what you may be thinking, Paul spoke directly to this issue. I want to give full content to the scripture, so we can be clear when we break it down. In 1 Timothy 4:5:3 (NKJV):

> 3 Honor widows who are really widows. 4 But if any widow has children or grandchildren, let them first learn to show piety at home and to repay their parents; for this is [a]good and acceptable before God. 5 Now she who is really a widow, and left alone, trusts in God and continues in supplications and prayers night and day. 6 But she who lives in [b]pleasure is dead while she lives. 7 And these things command, that they may be blameless. 8 But if anyone does not provide for his own, and especially for those of his household, he has denied the faith and is worse than an unbeliever. 9 Do not let a widow under sixty years old be taken into the number, and not unless she

has been the wife of one man, 10 well reported for good works: if she has brought up children, if she has lodged strangers, if she has washed the saints' feet, if she has relieved the afflicted, if she has diligently followed every good work. 11 But [c]refuse the younger widows; for when they have begun to grow wanton against Christ, they desire to marry, 12 having condemnation because they have cast off their first [d]faith. 13 And besides they learn to be idle, wandering about from house to house, and not only idle but also gossips and busybodies, saying things which they ought not. 14 Therefore I desire that the younger widows marry, bear children, manage the house, give no opportunity to the adversary to speak reproachfully. 15 For some have already turned aside after Satan. 16 If any believing [e]man or woman has widows, let them [f]relieve them, and do not let the church be burdened, that it may relieve those who are really widows.

From the above scripture just at a reader's glance supports what was said to me by my pastor at the time. However, when we really divide the word of truth and understand what Paul was teaching Timothy and the church, we see a few things missing from his interpretation. The first thing I would like to point out is why Paul approached the topic of widow in such an aggressive way. Paul was teaching and setting up order in the church. At this time there was an office setup for Widows. They were maintained by being employed by the church, this aided from the church. Their responsibility was to tend to the sick and the aged. This was set up because in Acts 6:1 Christians felt that the widows weren't being cared for properly by the church in a sense they were the neglected group. Paul goes on to first establish ground rules for those widows who are to be cared for by the church. He first says, "honor widows who are truly [indeed] widows. Now, when I read this, I was taken aback by the language. As we know Paul was a well-educated man, who spoke with intentionality. Paul uses the word "Indeed" or "Truly" or for other versions "Destitute" I believe understanding what Paul was conveying is to understand the person Paul was as a leader. Paul's foundation was for the church to make provision, or care for, or maintain the widow who has been entirely left alone, with no adequate income, one who trusts in God, only depending on the Lord for provision and who has dedicated her life to the ministry. He was clear, if the widow has no family, no job, no means of income to maintain her. Then Paul explains what qualifications she should have when a desolate widow comes in the number. Here is where the church takes the scripture out of context.

Paul goes on to say, if a widow is 60 years old, put her on a list to receive regular assistance if she is the following: 1. wife of one man, 2.reputation for good deeds, 3.she has brought up children, 4.show hospitality to strangers,5. if she has fed God's people, 6.assisted others in distress,7. has devoted herself to doing good in every way. Paul was setting the stage to support the mothers of the ministry that has lost their husbands. Now, Paul then says to the young widow - do not put her on the list for regular assistance because she will have the desire to marry again, and she might get lazy and comfortable with the church's support. Widowhood is a desolate state. Therefore Jeremiah 49:11 states, let the widows trust in me. After all that Paul wrote regarding widows and the church's provision for widows with how I was treated and the lack of understanding from leadership I came to realize that our modern churches are ill-equipped for widows. Not to mention young widows. Unfortunately, I was one of the young widows who had no one to lean on or depend on and fell into the extreme poverty category, became homeless, losing everything. I do believe if the ministry were set up to catch widows when they fall on hard times due to the loss of their spouse, whether through temporary financial assistance, education, mentorship, grief support, widow & widower ministries; this would provide help for a more effective bounce back and help start the healing process. When ministries are in position it also helps prevent widows from falling into the snare of trying to find her place in the world, and there would be less resentment from us in the church.

With the growing number of widows in the United States today there are about 40 widows for every church according to AARP, depending on the size of the ministry. There are widows in ministries that no one even knows are widows because they are the most displaced, overlooked, unattended-to group of people. Upon the death of a spouse along with feeling alone they lose about 70% of their support base that they had while married. This is the importance of churches standing in the gap. The loss of friends is due to the lack of understanding and unrelatable situation that the widow now finds herself in. Becoming a widow coach has enabled me to communicate with widows from all backgrounds, and age groups, who have expressed the unchanging disparities of widowhood. The consensus has been, no one will understand the position they are placed in on the day their husbands leave this earth. Widowhood isn't nor has it ever been a race issue or an age issue, it will always be a human issue that visits the homes of women across the globe. Widowhood should not feel like a natural death, but with the economic, social, and spiritual displacement, it sure can feel like it. It is necessary for us as a nation to stand with widows everywhere, bringing awareness to the disadvantages placed upon widows from the government, to our synagogues to organizations small and large. We as a people can change this by beginning to have these hard conversations in our ministries, communities, and families. Creating grief support groups that specifically address issues that widows face. Hire outside widow coaches that have walked that journey, who can speak power and life back into the widow and her family. Lastly, let us not speak about change, let us be the change which will have a lasting positive effect on every widow's road to healing. The goal isn't for her to just be healed but become a whole woman that will thrive.

Shaken & Still Standing

Widowhood isn't your death sentence. Although many days it felt like it, after almost 10 years on this journey I've realized, It's not personal, It's PURPOSE! Throughout my healing process I realized when I lost my husband, I'd lost myself, my passion to dance, preach, or even live. One day sitting at my desk while writing this book, it became clear to me, widowhood wasn't my death sentence. Indeed, I'd lost him, but there was so much more to live for. The fear of moving forward was the biggest obstacle I'd faced throughout this journey. It takes courage to pick up the pieces of your shattered life and make the decision to live. That's exactly what I had chosen to do. The moment I stopped fighting against the very thing that was the substance of who I am, was the moment I found joy in who I am becoming flaws and all. Yes, becoming a widow shook my entire world, and for a long time I truly believed that I would never love or laugh again. I knew I would never be the same, because that was a major loss in my world. Then I realized this wasn't designed for me to be the same. It was designed to show me sometimes God must shake up your faith to remind you that you are ultimately on solid ground. I was shaken, but I didn't break, I suffered a major loss, but it wasn't over for me. It became a part of my story that makes me authentically me. Growing in pain isn't always about learning something new, it is unlearning the old. Having the ability to shift how we think, our outlook on life, and our unhealthy behavioral patterns can control the speed of our growth process. We don't necessarily know where we are going but having faith to know that we are heading in the right direction and trusting the process is vital. Every season of our lives should reflect some sort of growth. I remember one summer I wanted to create an oasis on my patio. So, I decided to go all out. I planted beautiful tulips, hydrangeas and roses. Not long after, all my plants died. I was devastated because I wanted to become better at having a green thumb. I counted it all a loss and cleaned out the plant boxes, threw away the dead flowers and decided to keep the seeds that looked damaged just to see what would happen if I replanted them. I didn't have any expectations of growth. About four months later, which was another season, I walked out on the patio to find the bubs of the flowers sprouting through the soil and dirt. What seemed to be dead seeds in one season doesn't mean they won't bloom in another season. We must remain in a posture of expectation to grow. Replanting what seems to be dead seeds gave room for new flowers to grow because I re-planted it in new soil and waited. Sometimes in our state of loss we must reach back to that place where we found joy. Sit there for a while and wait while we heal. We will be able to see the evidence of our growth. Waiting isn't a bad thing; it is our lack of patience that makes it seem as if it is something bad that is happening to us. Posture yourself in expectation, knowing that while you are waiting God is healing every broken place, in the depths of your heart that man cannot reach. As He is healing you, He is growing you in grace, and that grace will be used to help others in their process of waiting, healing, and growing, it is the true definition of love. Fall in love with who you are becoming. Allow yourself the space and opportunity to grow. To find you, know you, and enjoy you. Living on purpose is so fulfilling but living God's way is even more fulfilling. So, I implore you, live God's way and discover who you are. Find your voice and fall in love with you again. Begin to charter your own path, embrace change, and dare to be different. No one ever said this road would be easy although we may want it to be, but believe me the journey is all worth it. No matter how long it may take you, remember your first love, what made you happy before you were married. All that made you happy before may not be what makes you happy in your new normal, but you owe it to yourself to begin to discover some things and gifts about you that you never knew were there. Being able to bounce back from the traumas of life, the things that have tried to kill me, and destroy what God was put on the inside of me, which was created to break strongholds, generational curses, and set people free; has truly been one of the greatest things that has ever happened in my life. To many that sounds crazy, but to genuinely smile again has been one of my greatest accomplishments because I survived to tell you that you too can and will survive. I had to make a decision to be intentional about living again, smiling again, or even getting out of the bed. Take small steps, then strides, then leaps. Embrace your process, but be intentional about moving towards becoming a better, new and improved you. I am still standing because I refuse to contaminate my future by holding on to the crisis of my past. I wanted to be healed and whole to be able to stand before millions and show them they too can overcome the traumas of their past. I fought for a long time against the call of God on my life to be a spokesperson for healing and change. I wanted to protect myself from experiencing the pain again, so I made my pain my God which almost killed me. Laughter at one point seemed impossible for me because of my depression. When I sought help, followed the blueprint for my healing, and committed to the process, my life changed right before my eyes. Now I laugh uncontrollably, I live unapologetically, and I love intentionally. This is the life we are designed to live. Yes, we will suffer loss, heartbreak, we will be discouraged, and sometimes feel like our life is coming to an end. But, once you make a mindset shift to live, you will begin to see yourself as the overcomer you always were. When trials come you will see yourself landing on your feet and having the ability to stand up straight. One of my daily affirmations has been "Lord, don't make my voice famous, make it effective" God makes no mistakes. He knows everything we will face in life; He also knows it won't always be good, but one thing for sure, it will work together for our good. It won't break you; you will not die in it. It will fortify you to become the person that was built to last.

Look at your future with confidence and peace and be postured with determination. Let that be your standard of living. Don't be afraid to rock the boat, greatness is always found beyond your comfort zone. Love doesn't always play out according to textbook standards. Love grows, develops, ripens, and matures on its own with patience, care, and nurturing. Love also has many chapters to search out, to explore, with much excitement, much to unlock, to discover, and unveil. Give yourself the time you need to love you and life again. Give it time to unfold. Open your heart to love and what it embodies. Don't measure it by others, don't hold yourself hostage to your past either. Be honest and true to yourself and allow God to rest in you and on you. Allow God to do what you are incapable of doing. Your healing and joy is locked up in that one decision. Forgiveness. Free yourself of whatever may be trying to hold you back from discovering your next you. Forgiving yourself will change the entire trajectory for your life. Maybe it isn't forgiving yourself, maybe it is someone else, whatever or whomever, doing it because your future self is waiting on you to live out your purpose. Be free enough to become who you want to be. Don't be hindered by the assumption that you owe your younger self or even your broken self a future that she has outgrown. Create the life that your future self is proud of. Possibilities end when you begin to put limits on them. Choose to live a limitless life. For many years I rejected being the face of widowhood, until that pivotal point in my life where I was either going to walk in the will of God or reject everything that he has in store for me. Was I afraid? Absolutely! Did I want to avoid this call of speaking and helping women rebuild their lives, most definitely. Like many of us, we want the beauty of the assignment, but rather detach from the pain of the assignment. Once I made my mind up to walk out the call and purpose God had for me it began to be revealed why I had to go through everything, from childhood until now. It was all about assignments. The greater the assignment the greater the pain. It all seemed unfair, and I carried, as mentioned earlier, "Why Me?" on my shoulders, but in all of that, I remembered that I was born for this very thing, it is not all for you, it is to pull someone else out of that dark place we found ourselves in. I am still standing to tell you that you will get through this, and God will show you your "Why?" Lean into your inner strength. You will find that you are more powerful, more impactful, more purposeful than you think. Search out who you are, what makes you happy, and what brings you joy. Then you will see a more defined way. Live, don't just exist. There is so much waiting for you to do, so many places for you to see, and so many more people for you to meet. Live to thrive in this new you.

Winning

While on one of my trips to Las Vegas I remember it was the last day of the conference, the team was in the conference room praying. At this point I was settled in what I received while here, the move of God was dynamic, but what I didn't know was there was more that God had in store for me. While on the floor praying and crying out to the Father, I remember, I heard God say "Get up and turn",immediately I got up and began to turn. As I started to turn I felt kinda weird because I did not know who was watching me, but the more I turned, the more I felt the presence of God surrounding me. I began to smile because I could feel the healing power of God all over me. I literally felt a touch go from the top of my head to my shoulders, to my waist, my legs, down to my feet. My heart was pumping in anticipation that something was about to happen to me. I thought to myself, what is this? Was I having a heart attack? The more I turned, I heard the people that were in the room crying in the background! I then heard God speak again "I'm Healing you, you will not cry any longer over this grief, I'm turning your mourning into dancing. I'm Healing you, I'm healing you, from the inside out, You will not go home with torment, You will leave here with Joy. Be Free Daughter." I turned some more, then I felt my smile getting bigger, I felt the hand of God, cleansing me, every part of me. It felt surreal. All of my anger, my sadness, the depression, all of my regrets were departing from me as I turned. God was healing me. I then felt myself drop to the floor, I heard God say! "No more tears, only gladness" I laid there with tears rolling down my face as I smiled. I knew from that point the tears had shifted! No more tears of sorrow, but tears of Joy! Joy because of what we shared, Joy because in Psalm 30:11 "You have turned my mourning into dancing, You have put off my sackcloth and clothed me with gladness" God is a healer! Yes you will cry! yes you will be angry, yes! you will feel like no one understands. But hang on in there a little while longer. God will heal you if you open your heart to Him. Allow God to go into the inner places of your heart that only He can reach. God is turning that dry sorrowful place into gladness. You will look back and rejoice because only you will know, without a shadow of a doubt that God is the one that brought you out of it. He Knows every tear shed. In Isaiah 53:5 "For He was wounded for our transgression, bruised for our iniquities, the chastisement of our peace was upon Him, and by His stripes we are healed" became the cornerstone to my testimony. I think about Chee-Chee, and always will, but, I am in a place where I can now smile, and cry but not mourn.

Where there is healing, there is freedom, peace, joy, and comfort to know that Jesus felt my pain! I didn't always see or feel that all I went through was in His plan for my life, but it has been shown to me through the process of time that it was and is working together for my good. Your process may be different from mine, your experience of needing God's healing may be different than mine, but I am sure of this one thing, if you stay the course and don't give up, it will work out for you. I believe God will heal your body, mind, soul, spirit, and your heart. It may not feel like you are winning right now. That's ok, keep pressing forward, change is expecting you. Your moment of shifting will come, just be ready when it does.

Putting Purpose on Pause

One day I asked myself these questions: Who was I without my story? Without the trauma, without the abuse, without the triggers of pain that I'd endured throughout my life? I stopped for a moment to reflect on who I was now? Here I was traveling the world helping people discover their true selves and realize I'd lost my sense of self. Not paying attention to the direction of my life had left me in a state of "Not Knowing" which became a place of uncertainty. I knew the obstacles I'd overcome were major milestones for me. I also knew I was identified as a survivor; but there was a piece of the puzzle missing. I couldn't put who I was into words without the back story. That was the moment I had to put my purpose on pause.

When trauma isn't dealt with it is buried. I developed the ability to identify my triggers by digging deep into the areas of my life I'd buried, with the burning desire to put a tombstone over them to solidify its death. The shock of becoming a widow was a trigger of the abandonment I'd faced years prior. It shook my world! I found myself in the midst of a storm without warning. With no plan of action I felt lost, confused, and extremely traumatized. I reverted to what I knew best, which was survival mode, but this time it was survival mode on steroids.

There is power in your decisions. Pausing for processing and healing. Making sure you're not bleeding out on others, tending to your traumas and disengaging from the cycle of pain is choosing you over your pain. Knowing who you are and your purpose is distinctly different than knowing you need to pause because you are bleeding out. To pause simply means to temporarily stop in action. For many of us, experiencing pain, loss, or failure can throw us into overdrive. I know for me, I found ways to keep busy to distract me from the issue that I may have been faced with. Ambition, while not censored or controlled, can be deadly. That seems a bit extreme, but allow me to explain.

When we experience pain, grief, or loss, of a loved one, a marriage, a job, or friendship and fail to acknowledge our pain or effectively process it, we can begin to bleed on others and our purpose. Then we find ourselves starting to function in dysfunction. We try to convince ourselves that everything will be fine if we stay focused on our business, our children, or even, drown ourselves in our self pleasing desires. That can range from spending frivolously, having unfilled relationships, starting friendships that we would not have started if not for that unaddressed grief.

Bleeding out no matter how severe can be controlled. When not controlled, it can lead to shock and even death. This is from the medical perspective, likewise, the same effects happen with the spirit. If we don't take a pause from the movement and address the emotional trauma no matter how big or small they may be- we have the potential of hemorrhaging, sometimes to the point where we become numb and dead on the inside. Controlling the bleeding is only one part of the process. There are a few steps you have to perform in order for the bleeding to completely stop. Let's explore the steps that I took in my process of putting my purpose on pause in order for my healing process to begin.

Applying pressure directly on the wound is one of the first steps to stop any cut, scar, or wound bleeding. Leaning into your wounds while they are fresh allows you to process all of those feelings while they are present. For me, I let too much time pass before I addressed my bleeding. As a result, I almost had a mental breakdown because I began to hemorrhage spiritually. I felt like all the walls were closing in on me. I pushed everyone away because when bleeding and in so much pain you do not want those who love you to see it. I remember, my children began to suffer from the effects of my pain. They were trying their best to be strong for me, but they were crying out because they wanted and needed their mother. They were the only ones who saw first hand whatI was going through. They saw I was in a fight for my life, and they were in no position to help me. They began to act out in school, they would cry at night, but I wasn't in a mental space to give them what they needed. I was totally withdrawn from even my very existence. Until the moment I realized I was dying. I made a decision to get help and really apply the pressure to my pain in order for the healing to begin. I started going to therapy, where I was able to explore the different pressure points in my life which contributed to the bleeding at what point I became withdrawn from life, and what traumas I had su for so many years. In essence these factors contributed to me not being able to handle life anymore. So, applying pressure and leaning in to those triggers and traumas will help you understand where you are, what you have not dealt with from your past, and in what areas you have to focus your healing.

The next step to pausing and healing is to evaluate your pain, and how much progress you have made from step one. After you have applied the pressure, examine your wound. By examining your wound, you have located the point of your pain, triggers, and unaddressed trauma. You will then establish the depth of your wound. How deep is the cut, how long have the wounds gone untreated, and what is the appropriate treatment for each wound. Some wounds may require less attention than others. This is the point where you identify and really be transparent and honest to why each wound was not addressed so true healing can take place. The only way healing can happen is to reveal your truth, and be resolved in knowing that you want to be better and be whole for you. The next step after examining your wound is to examine your heart. What is your heart posture towards that particular wound? Your heart posture may vary depending on the depth of the wound. In some areas you may not bleed out on others as much as you would for an area of trauma that has the depth of hurt connected to it. For example, losing my husband was the first loss that I'd ever experienced in my life. It was a wound and a cut that was so deep I became numb to the concept or thought of death. When my brother passed away I was so numb I cried one time, not because I lost my brother but because I had not addressed the unresolved pain of losing my husband, so the trauma felt so fresh as if it was my husband's death all over again. The result of not tending to my wound didn't allow me to mourn the death of my brother, because I was mourning the death of my husband again. Going and talking to my therapist allowed me the space to express the of losing my husband, and in those sessions I realized that I had not dealt with the of losing my mother to suicide. Not being able to hold her, hear her voice or knowing what she smelled like was the pressure point of my trauma pertaining to loss and grief. I was able to identify these pressure points through therapy and really being honest with myself and examining the blood flow of my heart posture.

Failure to examine the blood flow of your heart posture will position you to experience cycles of pain and create generational curses of emotional blood clots in your blood line. When you decide to take steps to become that curse breaker in your family and really examine the root of yourpain, you are deciding to give not only your children, and your children's children a fighting chance, but you are making a decision to pursue greatness in raw and broken form. In order to be great you have to be willing to be broken. This is the true meaning of putting purpose on pause. Once you have overcome the traumas and triggers of your past, purpose can continue to manifest in its fullest form for your life. When your pressure points are addressed and your triggers are identified it is then you will realize the bleeding has slowed down. When you continue on your healing journey and you realize that when faced with those same triggers with no response of pain but instead you respond in power you have been healed and made whole. Your scars in those areas have been healed and you are now able to move onto the next level on your healing journey. Take your time, this is not a race it is a marathon. You will reach the finish line, and in each lap you take you will see how much stronger you are becoming, how much more wisdom you are gaining, and you will begin to see your true purpose being revealed. The fear of success comes from continuing to carry the baggage of your past failures. It is your time to let it go and soar. Processing your pain allows you the opportunity to heal and live a more fulfilling life. Taking control of your healing will be the best decision you will make in your life.

What you are going through and have been through isn't really for you, it is to help someone else. It is up to us whether we want to take what we've learned and share it with others that may not have the skills and tools to overcome it. Or will you sit on the golden nuggets God has blessed you with. The choice is totally up to you!

God has an interesting way of sitting you down without permission. I fell ill which forced me to sit with myself, my triggers and with my trauma. It was then I realized I was masking my pain with working, attending church, and creating businesses. God spoke to me one day and said, *"Heal before you can be a conduit of my healing power. Allow me to heal you, so others can see their future in me through you"* It was at that moment, my eyes were opened to the understanding, most of us have the tendency to become busybodies in our brokenness. If we fail to put purpose on pause and make our healing a priority we will find ourselves roaming in the wilderness longer than intended. I found myself wondering and drifting further and further away from purpose each day, each moment, every second I spent away from pausing and sitting with God and myself. I was afraid of what the process of healing would look like for me. The process of grief for many can be very difficult. Adjusting to your new normal is even more difficult because you now have to create a life without your loved one. That person that you thought would've been by your side, through all of the Good, the Bad, and the Ugly.

The woman that stands before you today was the same woman who grew up motherless, came through the foster care system, a battered wife at the age of 20, divorced by 23, married again by 25 widowed by 30 with three children to care for as a single mother. Now! At the tender age of 41 I am a living vessel, proof that God does not call the qualified, with the perfect name, or background, but He qualifies the called according to His purpose. I am stronger today than I've ever been. I am better because I fought to be free from the generational bondage of those who came before me. I stand a little taller because I never gave up, even in the face of adversity. By remaining humble, and resilient, my faith grew to be unmovable no matter what comes my response will always be *"I will make it through this...too"* I encourage you today, Put Purpose On Pause and make your healing a Priority.

You have everything you need to overcome. Our lives aren't in any textbook, nor can it be broken down in any course outline. Our lives are designed and were written before we were born. On our healing journey we must remain vigilant in not staying on pause waiting for perfection. Nothing will ever be the same, and nothing will ever be perfect. Make sure you are conscious of not holding yourself to unrealistic expectations in order to force your healing or to be impactful.

If I could say anything to my younger self it would be, you're not losing, you're learning. I've learned throughout my journey there were moments I wanted to give up because life wasn't going as planned, or relationships may have not worked out the way I'd hoped, or a business venture I put my blood sweat and tears into, failed. I'd beat myself up, locked myself in a dark room and thought nothing would ever go right. All I needed to do was give myself grace, room to make mistakes, and patience. It would turn around and work in my favor. Take your time, be patient with yourself. Be encouraged, it will turn around for you. Tell your future self thank you for showing up as your best self. Thank you for being patient with me.

Life is getting better, even as you are reading this message. You do not see the results of it right now, or tomorrow, or even the next day, but believe me it is getting better. Seeds of hope, joy, and restoration are resonating inside of you. All it takes is for you to believe. I believe in you.

The next area I want to address is an area I see so often when faced with grief particularly. I found myself becoming so consumed with keeping myself busy in keeping Chee-Chee's dream alive where I became a walking shrine of who he was instead of living for me and representing what he stood for. I know this may hit home for many widows, but allow me the opportunity to break this section down.

It was very important for me to make sure Chee-Chee's vision stayed alive. I wanted to open up a school for music and the arts, I wanted his daughter to sing, play the piano, and drums. I wanted everyone to know what a contribution he was to this world by living out his dream. In the process of that I never paused to seek God to find out if this was a part of my purpose in life. I never stopped to think was this something that my daughter wanted for herself or that she even enjoyed. I knew that his vision could not die when he died. Now, here is the dilemma in this, was this God's will for my life, and what was the assignment for me as his wife and him as my husband. I knew there was something that was supposed to be birthed out of this but I didn't know what it was. So, by not putting purpose on pause, I became burnt out. Burnt out trying to live up to the expectation for his family that I was going to be the one to carry his legacy, trying to prove to myself that I loved him so much that I would dedicate my life to proving that his life was not in vain. That was a heavy burden to carry. I am not saying I wasn't up for the challenge, but I would be lying if I say it did not feel like the world was on my shoulders. I subconsciously took on a task that I wasn't sure I could carry out. Knowing our assignments and purpose can sometimes get clouded by circumstances and grief. This is why putting purpose on pause will allow you the time to regroup and refocus on your assignment. When we are grieving we tend to make decisions that may not be in our best interest nor in the interest of our future. So, slowing down, taking a time out, or waiting a little longer doesn't mean you've lost. It simply means that all things are coming together through the process of time.

It is our time to step up to the plate, posture ourselves to hit the ball out of the park. The moment you decide to keep living is the moment you accept that on this journey called life, there will be more good times, actually there will be times that you deem great. You will also experience some bad ones, and you will experience times that are absolutely ugly. The one thing I will say, it will all be worth it. Be resolved in your mind that you will not only live through this moment, but all the moments that are ahead of you. Utilize the strength within you; and in time, it will be made clear. It's all working out for your good. These intricate moments are designed to grow and develop you into what you were created to do here on the earth. When you come out on the other side of suffering, and you will. You will begin to see your purpose being revealed.

I came out of the hardest decade of my life, and I can now confidently declare I am "Walking in my winning Lifestyle" Your healing and Joy is locked in that one decision; Forgive. Free Yourself by making this decision which will change the entire trajectory for your life. Whether it is forgiving yourself, or someone else, do it because your future self is waiting on you to live out your purpose. Love doesn't always play out according to a textbook. Love grows, develops, ripens and matures on it's own with much patience, care and nurturing. Love has many chapters to search out and explore, with much excitement, much to unlock, to discover and unveil, give yourself time to unfold. Open your heart to love again. Don't measure it by others. Don't hold yourself hostage to your past. Be honest, be true to yourself and your heart's desires. Open your heart and allow God to do the rest. Allow God to do what you may be incapable of doing. Use common sense, counsel and wisdom. Through it all, never lose your hope or your beautiful smile. Don't be afraid to rock the boat; greatness is always found beyond your comfort zone. I am looking at my future with confidence and style. I am postured with determination. My desire is for you to do the same.

Live Again

Life after widowhood can be damn near impossible if you have not taken the necessary steps for your healing mentally, socially, emotionally, and physically. For some people living again may mean relocating to a new state. For others, it may take them selling their homes and moving into something new and fresh, or, it may simply mean changing the paint on the walls. To live again means something different for everyone. Let's keep in mind that I can give you the tools to help you start your journey of living again, but it's up to you to apply it, find your niche, and as I quote my business partner, Maya Tyler "Find what turns your light on".

The moment I made a decision to live again; I was preparing for work one morning and I heard a still small voice say "Pack". I knew it was God giving me instructions for my next move. That evening I gathered boxes and began to pack up the house. My children thought I'd totally lost my entire mind, but I knew what God spoke to me, and I was radical enough to trust wherever he sent me. Those boxes sat on our living room floor for over eight months. One Saturday morning my daughter came into my bedroom and said "Mommy, so are we leaving or what? God told you to pack this stuff but did he tell you where we are going yet?" I looked at her and smiled, responding to her truthful yet sassy statement "Yes baby, we are moving to Maryland very soon." She ran out of my bedroom with such excitement. I'm sure she didn't understand what that really meant for her, nor did she understand that the life I built for us here in New York, we were leaving behind forever. I knew deep within me, there wasn't anything left for me to complete here. My assignment was completed in this city. So I stepped out on faith and began searching for change.

Well, in a little over two weeks I started traveling back and forth between NY and Maryland looking for a place to live, and interviewing for jobs. That was a project within itself. I thought coming from NY with my experience, getting a job would be easy. Well, it wasn't. I was turned down for the best of jobs to the worst of them. I thought to myself was my resume not up to par? Was I not meant to move? Did I misunderstand God's word spoken to me? There were so many thoughts running through my head, but I knew God would always confirm His word to me. I remember one day speaking to my friend, and in the middle of our conversation she says "Vioree you just need a fresh start, away from here, away from all of this." She said "I know you believe and have a strong sense of Faith in God, I know he told you to leave, and when you do He will provide everything you will need." She isn't a Christian, but she was placed in my life to remind me of God's word spoken to me, and to encourage me in that moment.

For the next two months I continued to go hard, looking for work, a nice place to live where I felt safe, and good schools for my daughters because I knew my son was going off to college. One day, I received a phone call from a headhunter that viewed my resume on Indeed.com. She was very impressed and wanted to schedule an interview for a job in Maryland as a temp as soon as possible. I thought to myself, something is better than nothing. I jumped in a rental car, and drove down first thing that morning, interviewed and drove back to NY. Three days passed, I hadn't heard anything, so I thought this was another flop. Friday morning of the following week at about 7am, my phone rang. It had to be an emergency because no one calls me this early. I answered as I always did in my professional voice, "Hello, Vioree Brandon speaking" the voice on the end of the phone sounded soft and timid "Hello, good morning, How are you this is Kim from Kindhearted Staffing" I thought, oh she's calling early this must be good. I replied, "Hi, how are you?" She explained the job I interviewed for would like to bring me on as a permanent employee increasing the salary by 20k which I initially requested. I accepted the offer which meant I had to travel back to MD to onboard. I thought oh my goodness, I have a job with no place to live. I remembered looking at an apartment that I really loved in a military community. When I first visited the property, there were no units that would accommodate my family. I decided to go back and look again. I stopped in, and the realtor remembered me as soon as I walked through the door. "Hello Ms. Brandon" I was shocked, because it was about a month in between the time I'd last visited. I was happy she remembered me, as we talked I expressed to her I'd just accepted an offer here in MD and needed a place ASAP. She said, "Ok, let me check to see if anything opened up." I was praying like nobody's business at this point. She looked into her computer, and said "Oh we have a three bedroom, and it's brand new, new appliances, new carpet, new everything, let's go check it out".

I walked in and felt the peace of God all over it. I said "I will take it!" She said "you don't want to look around?" I said "Nope, I feel the peace of God in this place, and it's mine" A huge smile came across her face, she responded "Ok, let's sign the paperwork so you can move into your new place." Within two days my new job became a reality.

John graduated high school in August, I moved the following day. Our new started when I trusted God, stepped out on faith, and put action to the word He spoke to me. It didn't take years for this move to happen and work in my favor. Unknowingly, God had more for me than a new job, and a new home. He had love waiting for me to arrive and show up in my wholeness.

I worked at my new job for about eight months before I started to mingle with my co-workers. Everyday, entering into my office building, I saw this tall guy standing at the door waiting to open it, like it was his job to be the building's doorman. He said hello to everyone that entered. I never thought anything of it, other than, this guy doesn't have anything else to do but open the door for people every morning. One morning in particular, John was home from school and I wanted him to come to work with me. As we were walking up to the building I said to John "There is this weird guy that opens the door for everyone, just say thank you and keep it moving" he says "Mommy you don't like nobody do you?" with a smile on my face I said "boy just do what I asked, I am not trying to make any new friends". As we approached the door he wasn't anywhere to be found. We walked into the elevator, as the doors were closing, this big dark hand stopped them. I was startled and jumped back. It was the doorman. As he walked into the elevator he said "Good morning" with an English accent. I realized how tall he was, he had to be about 6'6' because he was towering over John. I said, "Oh, Good morning." I looked at this man from head to toe because I didn't realize he worked in the building. Later that week I found out he was the building Chief Engineer. Attractive was an understatement, but kept it cool because I promised myself, the next man I was interested in I would marry. This promise made me very cognizant of who I gave my time to which made me very intentional about my future relationships. I also was afraid of another failed relationship.

It was a Friday afternoon, all of my co-workers went out to have drinks and I decided to stay behind to catch up on some work. I looked up and saw the doorman walking on my floor, right by my desk. He stopped and says "Hello" I said "Hello Mr. Doorman" he laughed and we began talking. We talked for the remainder of the time my coworkers were gone. We exchanged numbers, with smiles on our faces and a glimmer of hope in our eyes. It was something different about him. I saw a sense of calm, peace, and the contraction of love.

For months we built a friendship. For the first time in my life, I decided to do something different. Some may say, I kept him a secret. But, I didn't keep him a secret, I protected what God was unfolding and what would be my future. I constantly thought, this is so different from what I've ever experienced in my life. The one thing that he did for me was allow me to speak openly about my deceased husband, and the feelings that I cherished with him. That for me was everything I ever needed. God gave me what I needed, and even more than what I wanted. I desired someone who had grace for me, and this man showed me that everyday with unconditional love and endless favor. As time went on, and our relationship blossomed, I noticed the relationship he developed with my children. There wasn't a day that went by that he didn't reach out to them independently of me. His relationship grew organically and uniquely with each of them. I remember praying one morning asking God, was I favored in His sight so much, that He would allow me to remarry after loss, and if this was who He designed for me, reveal the purpose in it. Months following that prayer God showed him and I things that were clear to our purpose together which was beautiful and would be beautiful in it's time of conception.

On May 15, 2021 I married an incredible 6'7" handsome chocolate brother. Fine, hard worker, Loves the Lord, and undeniably loves me and my babies. God was mindful of me.

For so many years I thought God forgot about me. I became complacent and comfortable with living with me and only me. I began to enjoy my singleness, my children, and fulfilling my purpose. Some may say, I suppressed my desire to get remarried. Especially because I was already in my second marriage and now widowed. Others may say I was just ok with not having a spouse and the responsibilities that come with it. For me, I wanted to do it differently this time. I wanted God to be all up in it. I wanted Him to hide me in the shadows of Him which would make it harder for the wrong men to see me and easy for the proposed one to find me. Later on in our relationship my doorman told me he saw me from one of the windows of the building, as he watched me day after day, he knew I would be the one he would marry. He understood he could not approach me the normal way, so he positioned himself in the right place at the right time in order to be noticed by me. So, he would watch me get out of my car, run to the elevator to make it downstairs in time to open the door for me just to say good morning. That made his day. There were times he missed the elevator, so he would walk past my desk to say hello. When I learned of all the energy, time, and dedication he put into trying to simply get my attention, I was floored. To this day he is proud to tell his story of finding his wife.

As I look at the chain of events leading to that very moment I realize God was ordering my steps. He knew what my winning lifestyle would look like. He wrote my story long before the world was created. Everyones winning lifestyle looks different, but the one common theme is choices. We all have a choice whether to live a life of depression, brokenness, and resentment or a life of purpose, love and happiness. The choice is up to you. Winning is not just another cliche or word to be thrown around because it sounds good. It is a lifestyle that is to be lived with no regrets. This is a lifestyle that everyone has the ability to live. It isn't just for the wealthy, or for famous people, or even those that we see flossing on social media. It is a real thing through affirming yourself, your purpose, and calling into existence everyday how you want to live.

Winning is what I choose when I wake up every morning. I speak over myself, my husband, my children, my finances, my future, and those things I want to see come to pass. You were born to win, your future was designed to be the evidence of winning. Your children and your children's children came from a lineage of winners. Being confident in this, sets the tone for you, when you are overcome with doubt. Those days will come. Days you don't feel your best, the days you struggle to even get out of bed, or the moments you feel like you are trying everything and nothing is working out. Remember, you are built to last. You were thought about before the foundation of the world. He

106

foresaw every emotion, every failure, every heartbreak, every disappointment, every moment that you felt rejected, abandoned, mistreated, used and abused. He saw it all, and God knew what you needed to get through those moments. He knew the very person to send your way to speak a word of hope. He also knew the exact person to give you a hug, or even bless you in the area of finance. That same God who knew then, knows now, where you are and exactly what you need, at the point of your need. Be patient. He hasn't forgotten about you.

While you are waiting for your situation to change, take this opportunity to work on your heart posture, work on sharpening your ears to hear clearly, work on your eyes so that you may have the ability to see as an eagle. Use this time to write short term goals (for the next six months) and long term goals (the next five years). Create an action plan for your healing. How do you see yourself as a healed, whole person? What would your life look like as a person that doesn't worry at the sign of failure? You can start your healing process right now. Your new mindset, attitude towards life and love starts right now. I believe in you!

Declaring & Decreeing My New Start NOW!

In this section I will give you a little insight of some of my daily affirmations, scriptures, and mantras that helped me get through the last decade. Also included are some declarations from my previous book "My New Starts Now"

I am humbled and grateful that you decided to take this journey with me! My prayer is that you will *NEVER* be the same. You are new because you have made the conscious decision to step out on faith, kick fear in the rear end, and move forward in being the best new you that God created. Remember, He has a purpose for your life no matter what your background looks like, no matter how many people think you are the "same old person", no matter how many times you may want to give up, no matter what mistakes you've made, you must always remember you are special to God. He always gives us the opportunity to become NEW in Him, and your new starts *RIGHT NOW!*

Let's begin by making some declarations over our day and our lives, which changes the trajectory of your destiny. Accepting the trauma you've faced by all of the wounds that tried to break you, and hinder you from moving forward has changed you forever. Your response to the trauma has the power to keep you stuck in a depressed, lonely, unfulfilling life or, it has the power to make your future a bright one. So, let's speak positive affirmations over your life that will help you pick up your bed and walk into living an abundant life!

I decree that today will be the beginning of something new in my life, which will flow out of me that will bring me Joy that I have never experienced before.

I decree, today will not be like any other day, It will be a day of recompense. It will be a day that I make amends with my past hurt and be rewarded for forgiving myself, and whoever has hurt me. My reward shall be a peace that surpasses even my understanding.

I decree, today will be a day that I am able to see my life through a lens of Joy, Harmony, and Oneness with God!

I decree, today I will fill my soul with positive thinking. All negative thoughts are cast down and removed from my mind.

Today is MY DAY! It is about me and my healing! I declare today to be ......(Put your name there) day.

I decree that today is a new day with the joy of God that will overflow from the depths of my soul! Lord, I ask that today You give me the ideas that line up with Your will for my life. Help me to make my life an example of Your living word working in me to advance the Kingdom of God.

I declare that every good thing You have promised me is MINE in Jesus' name!

I decree and declare great success over my life, my children, and every person connected to me according to Your will, in Jesus' name!

I decree and declare, according to your word in Psalms 115:12, that You are mindful of me, my children, and my ministry. I thank You Lord, that You love me and you gave Your precious son that I may have eternal life in You!

I decree that today I will write Your vision for my life and make it plain. Lord, today, cultivate that vision and my dreams to manifest in this life!

Lord, I decree and declare open doors for me today that will create divine connections that will advance the kingdom of God!

I decree and declare that every plan the enemy has set for me is destroyed by Your power, in Jesus' name!

I decree and declare that the works of the enemy against me are dismantled by the Blood of Jesus Christ.

I decree and declare health and wealth!

I decree and declare wholeness and freedom! I ask You, Lord, to awaken every dream and enhance every idea, in Jesus' name, Amen!

I decree and declare:
TODAY IS MY NEW DAY FOR MY NOW SUCCESS!

Made in the USA
Middletown, DE
22 April 2022